UNCERTAIN PASSAGE

First published in 2026 by
The Dedalus Press
13 Moyclare Road
Baldoyle
Dublin D13 K1C2
Ireland

www.dedaluspress.com

ISBN 978-1-915629-54-8 (hardback)
ISBN 978-1-915629-55-5 (paperback)

Dedalus Press titles are available in Ireland
from Argosy Books (www.argosybooks.ie) and in the UK
from Inpress Books (www.inpressbooks.co.uk).

Cover image by Holger Lonze,
by kind permission.
www.holgerlonze.com

Dedalus Press receives financial assistance from
The Arts Council / An Chomhairle Ealaíon.

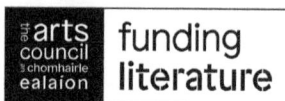

UNCERTAIN PASSAGE

PADDY BUSHE

DEDALUS PRESS

ACKNOWLEDGEMENTS

Some of these poems, or versions of them, were published in the following periodicals: *Archipelago, Cyphers, Howl, Poetry Ireland Review, Southword, The Dark Horse, The Stony Thursday Book* and *The Irish Times*

'A Vision in a Time of Disease' and 'Birdwatcher' appeared in *Local Wonders,* ed. Pat Boran (Dedalus Press, 2021).

'The Etymology of Isolation' was broadcast on RTÉ Radio 1, and also appeared in *Poems from Pandemia,* ed. Patrick Cotter (Southword Editions, 2020).

'Echoing Below' is part of a sculptural monument of the same name by Holger Lönze, which was commissioned by Belfast Harbour Commissioners.

Thanks to Bloodaxe Books for permission to quote from 'My Dark Fathers' by Brendan Kennelly from *Familiar Strangers: New & Selected Poems 1960–2004* (2004).

Contents

I

Accompanist

And it is now, when the accompanist
Lifts his eyes in anticipation towards

The singer, as towards a haloed figure;
Now when she, at the end of a familiar

Song in an unfamiliar language, utters
Herself into a note of such intimacy

That it resonates beyond all language;
Now when he, in perfect time, lowers

His poised hand across the centuries
To touch the strings of time and space

Towards an almost voiced translation,
Then closes his eyes with a tiny smile;

It is now the listening poet once more
Weeps for the meagreness of words.

Amergin in 2020

His soul bruised, his whole self buffeted
By the black winds he feels circling the earth,

His senses racked beyond themselves
By an acridity of smoke, an uneasiness

Of rising water, a blaring of loudspeakers
From those who drive fires and whose ships

Trade widely on spreading waters, he weeps
For the world he once uttered into being.

He weeps for the disarticulation of his vision,
For the self become solitary, for *us* and *them*,

Weeps for his *I* become *it*, for the hawk
Forlorn on the cliff, the salmon twisting

Desperately in rivers no longer familiar, weeps
For sun, moon and stars calculated to an abyss.

Knowing, however, no other words, he steps
Onto the shore once again, once again begins.

Tabula Rasa

after Arvo Pärt

The unending summons to begin.

Still that
Insistent
Emergence of bells, drop
Upon shapeless
Drop forming an idea
Of something that might
Ultimately chime, or toll.

Does listening create
What is heard? The sound
Bring forth the creature
Uttering the sound?

Urgent, then, the beating of wings, urgent
The guttural shaping in the throat, urgent
The smile or the snarl it decides to be.

The unending summons to choose.

Sheltering

I read about new weaponry, the old
Linguistic origins of *thermobaric*.

News channels repeat and repeat
Enumerations of the unthinkable

That I cannot absorb. I retreat
Into the familiar shelter of words.

A *target* – the diminutive of *targe* –
Originally meant a small, round *shield*,

A word that built itself into *shelter*
A shelter being a formation of shields.

When *target* galvanised itself into verb
It first meant *to shield, to offer shelter*.

No word of this nor any measured
Shift of meaning over the centuries,

Is of any significance at this moment
For those whose shelters are targets

Or for those others who are targeting
The sheltering basements of Mariupol.

Aerial footage pulses with digital circles
Fragmenting into outbursts of smoke

Above targets that had been theatres,
Had been hospitals, had been schools.

Meaning has sunk unfathomably below
Words, howling itself towards silence.

22nd March 2022

Vision

I can see him, yes, can imagine
Had he lived, the martyred one
Who once rode a winged horse,

See him, on his official balcony,
Green-shirted and high-booted,
Having just addressed his ranked

Followers in the bannered square,
See him lay aside for the moment
His staff of office, to ceremonially

Wash his hands in a cut-glass bowl
As the crowd surges in all directions
To seek out and identify all enemies

Of the nation and all calumniators
Of God and of the dead generations.

Sanctuary at Termonbarry

Pause here by the Shannon. Trace the name.
Tearmann roots itself in the Latin *terminus*:
A border, a limit, a territorial boundary stone.

Here Bearach, a sainted man whose staff
Was later used for cures, or swearing oaths,
Marked out holy ground at a river-crossing.

Trace how *tearmann* slowly unburdened itself
Of possession, glossing itself towards haven
Towards safe ground, towards protection.

Today the dictionary confirms that liberation:
A right of sanctuary, a place of refuge. Tradition
Refused right of entry only to carriers of plague.

> And let it shine its light today, this etymology
> That makes a boundary a crossing-point to safety.

Where the Words Bring Us

for Bernard O'Donoghue

(i)

Sometimes it's just the half-remembered
Words of a song that everyone half-knows

Will bring us out of doors: out of the kitchen,
Or the pub, even out of the drawing-room

With its arrangement for voice and piano.
So early one May morning we'll all rove out

And along the enchanted way we'll listen
To the thrush and the robin their sweet notes

Entwine, near where the maid and her lover
The wild daisies press, down by sally gardens

Long overgrown, then we'll roam the greenwood
To the Moss House where the birds do increase.

(ii)

It's there we will find it, we know sure enough,
Even though we're not sure what exactly it is

We're looking for, while the Moss House itself
Is just words in a song, an inscription on a map.

If we're lucky, we'll know where we should dig
To uncover the foundations, but we won't need

To dig to know they're there, because the song
Has told us what the place had told the song

Long before everyone half-forgot most things.
And we will stay still and listen and take the air

Of the place, and tune our ear and voice, that we
May sing a song that's antecedent to its words.

Language Loss

for Olivia O'Leary

In Irish, the ringed plover is a *feadóg chladaigh*,
And that shoreline whistling was what I heard

When the bird, piping distractively and feigning
A broken wing, did everything to draw me away

From the small, scraped-out hollow in the sand
Where she had laid her four pebble stone eggs.

For days, with binoculars, I watched her brood,
Saw her weave diversions against hooded crows.

She couldn't divert the storm, nor stay the tidal
Surge that levelled the beach and all its hollows.

Now and again I make out high-pitched snatches
Of a song in despairing search of its own words.

Eagle

i.m. Eibhear Walshe

(i)

Only here and there does the old roadway
Show itself through the overwhelming bog.

Here and there centuries of disuse relent
And allow hollowed-out passages or stone

Foundations lift themselves out of the heather.
A broken line, barely visible on the old map,

Goes astray in a tangle of roots, snagging itself
On rusted barbed wire fences before sinking

From sight as surely as it has sunk from memory.
Only on the higher ground, where the wind

Has flayed bare the shoulders of Mullach Beag,
Does the road again assert its sinewy strength.

(ii)

We have walked up through ruined settlements
Where generations had scraped out survival

Before the lakeside road below us was built.
Their hard-won houses and walls have long

Faded to anonymous rectangles on old maps.
Now, high up, as we approach Cnoc an Fhiolair,

Huge wings soar from their own extinct name
Over deserted townlands, like some descendant

Of emigrants getting to know the old territories.
Moving too fast for binoculars, that reintroduced

Sublimity passes overhead, loses itself in clouds.
We turn, trying again to decipher the old road.

Earth Singer

i.m. Seán Garvey

So you won't, as I think you always knew,
Make old bones. The otherworld, its lines
Etched on your face as it echoed behind
Your songs, will now be your daily haunt.

But you have travelled deep into the bones
Of that mountain that looks upon the sea,
And rowed out on *Cuan Bhéil Inse* to meet
Others whose songs are shaped by the earth.

And now you can make the same discoveries
All over again, without distraction, and know
The dewy freshness of *An Beinsín Luachra*
Blossoming into *The Bonny Bunch of Roses*.

Sing now, *a chroí*. With the earth's old bones
Your sounding board, sing *ón dtalamh amach*.

A Hare's Breath

Just as my kayak
Back from the island

      Noses towards the gravel
      Down from the carpark

A grazing hare raises
Its head to evening air

      Balanced on the instant
      Between flight and stillness

And yards from the landing
I slowly lift my paddle

      To drift between elements
      Inhaling the hare's breath.

The Lady and the Storyteller

for Seán Mac a' tSíthigh

It was in his bones before he was born,
The island mountain that had stretched

Itself lazily into the sea for centuries
Or reached mysteriously into clouds

In search of the old gossip and stories
That he then passed on to the islanders.

But when the lady, speaking *de très
Haut en bas*, and carefully marshalling

Every last weapon in her armoury
Of superiority, belittled the storyteller's

Mountain, along with all its imaginings
Through the generations, and explained

How valueless his old stories were
(even those told by the mountain)

How confused his languages were
(especially those she did not speak)

He drew her as a stick-doll, a cartoon
He carried from the base to the very

Summit of the mountain, where he let
The wind take it, then watched it drift

And diminish out of vision, accompanied
By the raucous mockery of seabirds.

The Duty to Dream

i.m. Merrily Harpur

A small cup with declaratory handles and base,
Elaborately shaped and smoothed from tinfoil,
Was how, twenty years ago, you formally steered

The poetry festival (that you had dreamt into being)
In my temporary direction, an untypical seriousness
Keeping you untypically subdued until you intoned

The accompanying inscription: *a poisoned chalice.*
That was when the whole room fell apart laughing,
As did your serious self. Until, that is, you urged me

To clarify for Mr. Heaney that it was *simply his duty*
To read at Strokestown International Poetry Festival.
Twenty up-and-down years, and each year the dream

Redreams itself awake, stretches itself into summer
And rises to welcome words and shapers of words
With lambs and bluebells around Strokestown House.

Now you have accepted, in all seriousness, your own
Poisoned chalice. I touch the strings of your name,
Imagine high rippling laughter, just beyond our range.

March 2025

Lines Written after a Poetry Festival

for Gillian Clarke and David Thomas

No, I didn't write today. I was catching up
In the vegetable garden, trying to untangle

Weeds from crops, roots from creepers,
All that rampant growth demanding order,

Demanding choice. I chose the rhubarb,
Exposing crowns that were lost in weeds

And decay. With a rusted but still springy
Four-pronged pike, I spread the manure

My farming neighbour brought me last year,
Crumbling, well-rotted, as it's meant to be.

Laying the wormy dung on crowns that held
Tiny, pink successors within, I wished them

Warmth through the winter, and a plenitude
Of time to contemplate spring unfurlings.

And I thinned carrots, betwixt and between,
As always, about what should be discarded,

Hoping the cull would let the others flourish
And swell out to fill the spaces in the lines.

November 2021

Castlebar Honey

with gratitude to a hive of Glenisland cousins

'If you are saying poems tonight,' smiled Mustapha
In *The Olive Tree*, where Tony brought us for a bite

Before the reading, 'then we must feed you honey.'
His words still hummed to me in the upstairs room

Where greetings buzzed among a swarm of cousins
Gathered, they laughed, for once without a funeral.

And after harpstrings and whistle-notes infused
Sweetness into every last corner of that room,

I dared to imagine that the words I was reading
In their turn flowed like honey, were mellifluous.

November 2022

For Jan Metz at Eighty

Skellig Michael, say, the barely worded
Fragments of its history in the annals
Animating the conversation of visitors
Bobbing in the swell below its cliffs.

Words, when all is said and done, are what
Remain, those that are heard and those,
Like melody, sweeter for being unheard
Even as they echo down grateful memory.

Or a group of scattered friends gathered
Now and then, here and there, to celebrate
Poems they have read and heard, voicing
A past and future that is always now.

And so, dear fourscore connoisseur of words,
Speak on, and may each word still resonate.

The Lambs at the Poetry Reading

I celebrate the darkness and the shame
That could compel a man to turn his face
Against the wall, withdrawn from light so strong
And undeceiving, spancelled in a place
Of unapplauding hands and broken song.
—Brendan Kennelly, 'My Dark Fathers'

At the festival reading in Strokestown House,
Its balanced architectural proportions a paradigm
Of rational self-interest, the famine-haunted lines
Wouldn't stop whispering their right to be present.

I tried to shush them, telling them that now
Wasn't the time, that I must give all my attention
To Aonghas Dubh's poem about his new-born son's
Beul beag hungering for life and words and song.

They insisted that here was exactly the place,
And that I must make the time to recollect that
When winds of hunger howled at every door
She heard the music dwindle and forgot the dance.

As the poet read, three lambs – it being May Day
They were still small – came to the elegant, sunlit
Window behind him with mouths full of bluebells
And grass, peering in curiously. The room cheered.

Somehow, between that reading and the harp music
That followed, I made time to listen again to the lines.
Somehow – and this is not rational or proportional –
The hands applauded once more. Song was renewed.

The Poet, the Painter and the Waterfall

(i)

Wide-eyed, transfixed, the poet stood
And watched. Under his astounded feet
Clay and rock heaved and thrummed.

What was it, this water overtumbling
Into such a continuum of light that fall
And rise became one and the same?

How was it, he asked, that the whole
Cascade of sound held within itself
The single, continual note of a bronze

Trumpet imposing order, that the light
Refracted through mist purpled itself
Around the high peak, like incense?

Like opening buds, then, answering lines
Poured down in constellations, silver stars
That pinned him to the welcoming earth.

(ii)

And this was where the painter, ages
Later, observed him working at words,
Stringing them like lights up and down

The height of the waterfall, star-showers
Flinging themselves above and beyond
Their known orbits, their ordained paths.

How would he paint this, staying fixed
To the earth like the poet who long ago
Disappeared into the stars he imagined?

Brushing himself deep into earth and sky,
The painter sprinkled those falling stars
Onto his closed eyelids, chose his tools,

Brought woodblocks of mountain cherry,
Mulberry paper and bamboo brushes,
Arranged his chisels and grouped his inks.

Then he gouged the water deep and wide
Into the wood, brimming over borders,
Upending planes, printing new horizons.

after Hokusai's woodblock print of Li Bai at Lushan Waterfall

Pipers in the Cave

for Maitiú Ó Casaide

1. Leaves from Lost Books

When your sonorous drones plumbed the depths
And Róisín's voice scaled the poignant heights

Of loss and learning in *Amhrán na Leabhar*,
Tomás Rua's grief was recreated as sweetness,

Pages from his books floated like counterpoints
From the Liberator's sunken boat in Derrynane,

Valentia rediscovered itself as Béal Inse, and threw
A bridge over *góilín aoibhinn Dairbhre* for the poet.

Here was restoration, and here was recognition
Beneath the drill marks shaped by calloused hands

That had shaken the hand of a poet of their own.
Tonight, the cave echoed his heights, his depths.

2. Her Secret Name

And when you and Ailean Dòmhnullach played
Ar Éirinn Ní Neosfainn Cé hÍ, drones and chanters

Fingering every crevice of those quarried walls,
The air itself lifted, there and then swelling

To fill all the space beyond us. Tiny stalactites
Gleaming on the cave's roof stirred themselves

To throw off the layered aeons of slate above
As they chimed to the music's exquisite probing.

Were there words to Ailean's singing voice?
If there were words, what language did he sing?

No matter. We held the meaning of the music
In our applause, our exaltation of her secret name.

Valentia Slate Quarry, 24th June 2023

Li Bai in his Garden

for Michael Harding

The old poet rests, no longer
Trying to make sense of it all.

Behind his closed eyes, troops
Of old friends gather, bringing

Wine and music, pouring both
To accompany impromptu lines

Invoking the shadows invited
By a huge, overflowing moon.

The poet smiles, recites in his turn
What he recalls of that plenitude.

A blackbird begins to bubble up
Its own tune from a nearby branch.

Li Bai opens his eyes, picks up
The flute he had put by his chair,

And plays a response to everything
He hears, everything he remembers.

Startled, the blackbird flies away,
Carrying a tune taken off the wind.

Heaney at Carnota

for Antonio Raúl de Toro Santos

It was when you recalled him stretching out here
On the grass beside the *hórreo*, its ornate pillars

Uplifting the airy stone granary, it was then
I sensed how much he must have felt at home

Here. Even with the carved granite elaborations
He must have loved this inhering rootedness,

Loved the white horse pulling the long stretch
Of its tether towards him, muzzle dripping grass.

I conjured then the broad rotundity of his vowels,
His scythefuls of edged consonants falling in rows:

> *Let me not, I pray, relinquish my grasp of such*
> *Places of stone, of stored grain, of meadows*
>
> *And meadow flowers, of this columbarium*
> *Echoed in* A Igrexia de Santa Comba *close by,*
>
> *All invoking Colmcille to spread his gentle wings*
> *In pilgrimage from the home place, and fold them*
>
> *Near this white horse, for all the world the same*
> *That nuzzled love at the saint's own deathbed.*
>
> *Let me not ever waver in this, nor let this warm*
> *Amplitude ever waver from its dear embrace.*

Carnota, April 2025

35

At Cill Ó Buaine

for Nóirín Ní Riain

(i)

At Cill Ó Buaine, the probing roots of furze
Have subverted the stone-paved terrace

And split the gable-shrine whose carved
Round opening gifted pilgrim fingertips

A fleeting brush with venerable bones.
The stones of the oratory are held now

By the woven grace of ivy. A cell doorway,
Still standing, faces neither out nor in.

(ii)

Yet still that sightline out towards Sceilg
That once embraced the celebrant emerging

From where he had embraced mystery,
Embraces me. And that other line of sight

Still draws me through a gap in the hills
Across the bay to An Lóthar, its ruined

Oratory and cross also facing the island,
Triangulating the land and sea for Christ.

(iii)

The lines of sight intensify themselves,
Clarify themselves as pure vision.

Now a light beyond time, beyond belief,
Animates the hills and gilds the ocean

That stretches towards the distant island
Clinging to the horizon's shifting planes.

Here now are bells, voices lingering in prayer
Upon prayer for the redemption of memory.

Naming the Rock

Scelec. That's a blade
Of sound, a slivered
Name to slice wide
Open my shrunken soul.

Far below, my brothers
Raise hands in a last wave
As together they row
Landward into my past.

Envisioning slabbed steps,
Quarrying my imagination
For cells, an oratory, hours
Punctuated by small bells,

I track the paths that rainfall
Will uncover, and I divine
Where God ordains I place
The slate cistern I will fashion.

A horizontal seam of quartz
Tracing itself through the rock
Gleams with the possibility
Of a platform for prayer.

Around me are absolutes.
Dizzy falls, but also summits
I can aspire towards. *Scelec.*
Upon this rock I will build.

Echoing Below

Go below. Attune yourself to the slow rise and fall
Of creaking planks, the rhythmic knocking of hulls
Against each other, the tug of hemp rope looped
Around bollards, furled sails lifting in the breeze.

Step ashore now. Admire the new quays, the civic
Order along the shoreline. Observe the unloading
Of Indian corn for famished hinterlands, the loading
Of fine linen for London and Dublin drawing rooms.

Go deeper then, and farther back. Feel the oozing
Marshland salted and shaped by channelled tides.
Know the sandbank that named this city. Absorb
The call of wading birds, the stirrings of mud crabs.

And after this immersion in brined and silted time
Open your whole self and senses to where you are.

II

Flame

for Prem Timalsina

After your video call from Kathmandu
Had stirred me from post-Covid lethargy
Once more into the wide, wide world,

I closed my eyes to see the flickering
Votive lamp Pramita and you have lit
In Swayambhunath for my recovery.

It all tumbled back then: the long, stepped
Climb to the high temples, the monkeys
Scampering from legend into sanctuary,

Intricacies of stone and wood and metal
In endless, exultant search of the source
Of that whose only source is its own being.

Imagining myself into the absorbent eye
Of a deer glimpsed through leafy branches,
I watched the sunwise circling of pilgrims,

Heard the murmured rhythm of their prayer,
Saw myself and my wide-eyed camera trying
To take in all this down-to-earth exoticism.

Now here's a down-to-earth exotic: one flame
Among the many tended to by the monks
At Swayambhunath is burning now for me.

And so I send my gratitude to you and yours,
The far and fragrant light of whose offering
Has drawn my befogged mind *deiseal* again.

The Etymology of Isolation

No man is an Iland, intire of itself.
— *John Donne*

I

Outside our window, above the wind-flecked
Bay between its two enclosing headlands,

A dozen gannets wheel, now and then plunging
And struggling up to wheel and plunge again.

I am contemplating *isolation*, its meanings
In the here and now and then and again,

Contemplating that *isolate* shares its Latin
Island roots with *insulate*, that each one is also

A peece of the Continent, a part of the maine.
Isolation warms itself towards insulation.

II

I think of our son, whose house on the small
Peninsula across the bay I can just make out,

Who drives with food and news and comfort
To our insulated door, like a boatman judging

A quick now or never surge to a storm-isolated
Island slipway, quickly heaving up supplies

44

One-handed, the other on the tiller steering
A curve astern. He smiles, waves. Half-joking,

Wholly grateful in this semi-isolation, I offer
A coinage: *peninsulated*. We'll live with that.

March 2020

Coronavirus Sculpture

Latin corona, a crown, a garland

(i)

Between one morning's bleak, isolated
Shoreline walk and the next day's tentative

Spring in the air and in my step, it appeared
Just above the tidemark, below the clay cliff

That's still eroding day after day, collapse by
Small collapse. And it just appeared there

As if the tide had stranded the whole thing
Or the choughs throwing their airy, corvine

Shapes overhead had danced its presence here
With a ceremonious scarlet and black welcome.

(ii)

Someone has gathered these stones, these shining
White stones, hundreds of them, gleaming in all

Shapes and sizes, enough to string a beaded wall
Around this weathered and tide-battered boulder

Shouldering its worn grey bulk out of the gravel.
I can see an old monk telling his beads, see a herd

Circled tight around its young. The ring of white
Quartz blossoms and settles. Here, now, is a corona

That will garland the fragile heart. And I would love
To know who built it. And I would love who built it.

March 2020

Reflections

(i)

The morning sun slants warmth along the beach,
Breath by breath, as delicately as a heron's slow

Angular steps between clumps of seaweed gleaming
On tide-washed rocks. The heron stops, straightens,

Stretches its long neck. The world is a water-bead,
The man on the beach a reflection in the heron's eye.

The woman at a faraway clifftop, who has paused
On her isolated way home from a Covid test

To take pleasure in the gannets wheeling offshore,
Is a reflection suddenly welling in the eye of the man.

(ii)

And that was then, and this is some uncounted days
Later and the test is negative, probably falsely negative

Your doctor says, but it makes not a blind bit of difference
Because whatever it was or wasn't you have come through.

At my laptop, I google the words of *Te Deum*. Unanswered,
I close my eyes. I recall that morning, that dead-still heron,

And I see its ragged grey and black outline transfigured,
See the bird robe itself in a crane's hieratic whiteness,

See the ceremonious outspreading of wings, see it lift
Itself, gracefully, towards some high and sacred space.

April 2020

Birdwatcher

for Seán Lysaght

For half a century I have lived
On this clifftop, and yet

Only now, over these last
Fully locked-down weeks,

Did I to angle a telescope
Onto the gaping beaks

And voracious red throats
Of four fledgling ravens

Nested precariously
On a grassy ledge close by.

I see too just how accurately
Flocks of tideline sanderlings

Can anticipate the speed
And reach of shore-waves,

Their precise, scurrying lift
And flutter, the probing beaks

Punctuating every advance
And retreat. And if I live

Long enough I will learn
To recognise how its size,

As well as the long downturn
Of its bill, helps to distinguish

The curlew, a threatened species,
From the whimbrel, which is not.

April, 2020

Nesting

for Mark Roper

A week after Brigid's day, and a pair of ravens
That have been throwing their high-five shapes

All over the wind-tossed sky, are perched now
On stakes above a tiny ledge in the clay cliff

Where their ragged, branchy nest overhangs
The tidal collapses and accretions of a year.

The nest that they – or theirs, who knows? –
Built last year, lies scattered where it fell.

We watched it through that lockdown spring,
Watched the young of those birds of ill omen

Open the beaks of their need until they too
Fledged, then dared themselves to the wide

Corners of shore and sky, of fields and hills.
Vulnerably ominous, they croak as we pass

Below, grateful that we – and ours, for who
Could have known? – can see them build again.

February 2021

A Vision in a Time of Disease

for James Harpur

The story may strain belief, but maybe no more
Or less than many others. In any case, a *Vita*

Relates how one saintly monk was consumed
By compassion for a youth whose life was blighted

By disease, and who had come in desperate search
Of a miracle. In pursuit, then, of his own salvation,

The monk took unto himself the youth's infection,
Thus healing him. It further tells that, years later,

With the name of having lived with the disease
In holiness and fortitude in the service of others,

The monk petitioned his abbot for a dispensation
To make a *peregrinatio* to Rome before his death

That he might pray before its relics and altars
And walk among its columns and sunlit squares.

But the abbot, seeing the ravages of the disease,
And fearing the added danger of travelling abroad,

Demurred, forbidding it with the full authority
Of his office. Being, nonetheless, a kindly man

Who saw the consternation his words had caused,
He bade the weeping monk lay his head in his lap.

The monk did so, and when, hours later, he awoke,
What traveller's tales he had brought, from Rome

And from eternity, and from even further abroad!
These he related to the abbot and to the monks

Whose hearts and souls had pitied their brother
And who now gathered around, all agog to know

How he had found, in the lap of the here and now,
The only heaven they would ever know, or need.

February 2021

Oratory

(i)

It's your oratory, the archaeologist joked
About the high ridge and pointed-arch gables

On the brand-new polycarbonate greenhouse
That had been our Covid summer project.

And yes, you could see a silhouetted echo:
Gallarus, say, or Cill Ó Buaine. We laughed.

Later, as I barrowed clay into raised beds,
And sunlight prismed itself into the interior,

I imagined a *scriptorium*, an illuminated
Manuscript of a *vita* lived in saintlier times

When work and prayer in unison conspired
Against the plagues ordained by god or man.

(ii)

Now our seedling spring onions are uncoiling
Their bowed heads from the clay. Salad leaves

Are raising themselves to embrace the light,
And I have planted garlic to overwinter here,

Placed each clove deep and firm to guard
Against the dark, to purify the blood in spring.

True, our oratory runs from north to south
And not from Christ's risen sun to its setting.

But heaven knows we had lost track of that axis
Years before we knew its orientation. So now,

Along our raised beds, *laboremus* at our ease,
Oremus as we choose, *et nunquam timeamus.*

III

Consultation

Again this morning the sun rising
From behind the frost-bound gloom

Of Cúm a' Chiste gilds the still bay
Silvery blue, burnishes the copper

Fronds of kelp draped over the rocks
And calls my world once more to order.

Again, I walk to the edge of the cliff
And sit beside the garden Buddha.

Out from the beach, the flat-calm sea
Scintillates, reflective beyond belief.

There is no need for the binoculars
To see the seals, arched and stretched

In twos and threes on low-tide slabs.
But when I focus, I can see their heads

Turn, those storied eyes reading mine.
I see them too through the uncertain lens

Of yesterday's meeting in the hospital
Consultation room. I have not yet found

The words to translate what our eyes read,
Each deep in the other. But I have learned

That stories will continue to be told
And tides will rise and fall as is ordained.

January 2024

The Intensive Care Unit as Rainforest

I know now, of course, about the residual
Morphine seeping the length of my spine

Like sap rising in trees. But equally, I know,
For hour after timeless, crepuscular hour

The ward hummed and pulsed and whistled
Itself into rainforest, wings flashed emerald

Or red from one branched and tendrilled bed
To another, calling out warning or reassurance

Above the rhythm of invisible cicadas, while I
Was still migrant, a bird of uncertain passage.

The Wisdom of Poets

for Lorna Shaughnessy and Mark Roper

Wise woman you are, Lorna, who foraged out
And sent me Mark's *Beyond Stillness* to quicken

Me into healing. And wise words of yours, Mark,
Who alchemised those chemotherapeutic terms

Into the radiant, redemptive stoop of the divine
Imagination transforming malignant cells towards

Whatever will be. Here indeed is plunging, here
Soaring to quicken and stir my heart in hiding!

From my still reeling hospital bed, I scan horizons
For words of gratitude towards the wisdom of poets.

Planting Alders

Yesterday, I planted trees. For years
I had resisted it. Trees take so long
To mature, it didn't seem worthwhile

Those early years. And the salt gales
That regularly flay our clifftop garden
Would, winter upon winter, I knew,

Insist on stunting them, so that spring
After spring would see the blackened
Tops of branches surrender, and sprout

Only below the parapet of the hedge.
But yesterday, I put down a dozen
Alders. They love the boggy ground,

And the hedge, not trimmed anymore
But taking its shape from the wind
And the weather, offers some shelter.

So I cleared grass that's no longer lawned
Into submission. And I spread the bared
Roots of the saplings around the oozing

Bogland that's layered on the glacial clay
Of our clifftop holdfast. First a robin, then
A thrush eyed the upturned soil for worms.

I let them at it awhile, then heeled down
The soil, and spread a votive covering
Of dung from my neighbour's cows on top.

They seem to have taken, tiny leaves today
Tenderly hopeful. In my seventy-fifth year,
I know the time is right for planting trees.

April 2023

Circuit

for Sinéad McElligot

What triggers the flashback, I think,
Is the narrowness – less than two feet –

Of the taped path around the perimeter
Of the gym that our *Better Bones, Better*

Balance group is walking, our weekly
Scramble in the face of encroaching age.

It has been the usual exercises, all more
Of the reassuring same, when the physio

Tells us to close our eyes for a few steps
To test our balance. I do so, precariously,

And all at once it is thirteen years ago
And I am walking The Annapurna Circuit

In a late monsoon. Where we have begun
The climb from lower ground, a huge

Mudslide, more than a hundred feet across,
Has blocked the way. The world heaves.

Villagers hurrying along the narrow path,
Beaten across the steep, unstable slide

By the sandalled feet of necessity, urge us
With wheeling hands and pointing fingers

To cross quickly, without pausing;
Another landslide is looming.

I tremble at the absoluteness of the drop
One slip would mean, the appalling roar

Of the torrent below, the imagined roar
Of an avalanche from above, before we

Traverse rapidly, booted feet outstepping
Our fear, to the firmness of stone again.

I open my eyes and continue the circuit
Towards the final balancing of bones.

Just Now

Just now, this minute, as I strain
   And stretch stiffened shoulders
As programmed by the physio,

I glance out the window and see
   A wagtail, then a robin, then a wren
Flit each in turn to a heap of grass

To bob and pick, bob and pick,
   Easing the morning's passage
Into day, just now, this minute.

Birthday Poem

Unimaginably, the biblical
Lifespan, and two for luck.

I measure out my morning
Tablets, spoonfuls of coffee.

The carcinoma on the back
Of my hand has been excised,

Biopsied. With eyes rinsed
Lucently clear of cataracts,

I see Carraig Éanna plainly,
Where, with my grandson,

Just a few days ago,
I kayaked, and landed

And clambered up
To wave to the wide world.

Soul, clap your hands
Louder, and louder sing.

August 2020

Towards a Bronze Sleep

This self-embrace, with one arm curving
Back along my cheek to grasp a shoulder

And, perhaps, the stars, the other drowsily
Exploring the comfort of downy pillows,

One leg stretching out towards memory,
The other raised to step into an emptiness

That becomes ever more substantial, this
Sculpts me nightly towards sleep. And this,

Incrementally, night upon night, has now
Been touched by some unnameable light.

Without agency, without volition, I absorb
Unmovingness, slowly hardening into bronze.

Stone Seal

Gleaned from the high-tide shingle on the beach
Below our house, it rests now on the windowsill
Beside my desk, grey sandstone flanks seamlessly
Curving up to form a raised tail, a watchful head.

The seam of quartzite it perched on, aeons ago,
Mirrors the wavelets just breaking on the rocks
Offshore, where seals have just now hauled up
To bask for however long today's tide will allow.

The Way It Should Be

The way it should be, really,
Is that the tiny, stone-built
Harbour is just a short way
Downhill from the house
You have in good time chosen
So that the sound of the tide
Rising and falling lifts itself
On the wind to your open door
Where you sit inside, reading.

Your boat, tarred, carvel-planked,
Its high bow broad enough
To shoulder off a choppy sea,
Should be tied bow and stern,
Her mooring arranged so that
She can be pulled alongside
Easily, no matter how high
Or low the tide may be running,
And boarded from the stone steps.

Ideally, an arrangement of bells,
Each with its own cherished note,
Will be in place, to let you know
In good time when you must go
The conditions you should expect.
If you are fortunate, harbour seals
Will accompany you, sleek heads
Coaxing your bow towards some
Uncharted point, just out of sight.

IV

Brushstrokes into Syllables

in response to paintings by Becky Munting

Barn Owl
The roosting barn owl
Contemplating uprightness
Might well be Buddha

Ravens
Grav gravitas grav
Gravitas gravitas grav
Grav gravitas grav

Robin
When a robin sings
From a bare branch in winter
The season's heart glows.

Hares
Since they are tricksters
If two hares sit back to back
Which is the other?

Pied Wagtail
He does bow and scrape
For food, but nevertheless
Waits on nobody.

Goldfinches
Goldfinches flitting
From branch to branch in the hedge
Illuminate us.

Blue Tits
Clinging for dear life
To the feeder, two of them.
Rhapsody in blue.

Wren
Such a miniscule
King of all birds! But just watch
How he struts his stuff.

Bullfinch
Bullnecked alpha-male
Puffed with masculinity.
But his breast is pink.

Goldcrest
Irish calls the bird
Lasair choille: a sudden
Flame between the trees.

Swallows
Such ease of movement,
Those migrants! But they twitter
Where is home is where …

Tree Creeper
Rely on these birds.
They will do exactly what
It says in the name.

Stag
I know my status
Blood and breeding. Forever.
Who or what's Landseer?

Sparrowhawk
In any language
To name victims in your name
Is beyond all words

Blackbird
So ordinary
Yet still incomparably
The sweetest of all.

Jays
To other corvids
They're somewhat ostentatious.
Not really the thing.

Fox
A fox stares at me
Dares me to stare back, to go
Where I dare not ask.

Garrán a' tSáile

Garrán a' tSáile
I called it, for the salt wind
That often flays it.

> I circle young trees
> With pikefuls of rotted dung
> Spreading it *deiseal*.

Oak, alder, holly
Send roots with long memories
Deep into the bog.

> Wild garlic sharpens
> The edge of that sudden smell
> On the zigzag path.

Sycamore leaves lift,
Silkily, like parasols
In a passing breeze.

> Branches overhead
> Meet secretly to narrate
> My father's stories.

Yes, it's a cliché,
But this sunny woodland path
Delights in dapple.

Goldfinches swaying
On seeded stalks are turning
Kaleidoscopic.

Cosán Éibhir, named
For our daughter's son, is now
Finding its own way.

When they feel exposed
I tell young beech that the path
Is an avenue.

From the garden seat
Summer leaves block my vision
While deepening it.

Here, deep in the shade
Of midsummer foliage,
Enlightenment gleams.

I am no hermit
But leaves stirring in the breeze
Whisper temptation.

First of April Walk

A shimmering sea.
They say the forecast is bad.
You could have fooled me.

> Sand martins whizzing
> Into their old nesting-holes,
> All over again.

A heron swings up
And, banking, loops to the shore.
Skateboarder of air.

> The raven brooding
> On its precarious nest
> Call this mindfulness.

You might call me old.
I think I'll live forever.
Who's the April fool?

A Rolliflex on Sceilg Mhichíl

in response to photographs by John Minihan

Here, at this distance,
This height over gilded waters,
What does *mainland* mean?

> A stone doorway leads
> One way or the other to
> Liminality.

Life/death, heaven/hell,
Saved/damned. Here's the whole thing
In pure black and white.

> The South Peak rises
> From stratum upon stratum
> Of stony-faced time.

Reaching the terrace
The steps can now tolerate
The horizontal.

> When the high cross fades
> At dusk, gravestones in the *leacht*
> Raise their arms in grief.

The high cross is stone
But often makes its slow way
Through the enclosure.

> Here each hammered stone
> In its ordained course can hear
> All the spheres chanting.

Windchimes

for Fiona

From an alder branch
My love, to help my healing,
Suspended windchimes.

                                    From this golden bough
                            They sing to those who pass now
                                        And then. And again.

Amidst the branches
Bared by winter, they give voice
To the silenced trees.

                                    For *path* now hear *aisle*
                            And for *garden bench* now hear
                                        Auditorium.

Each and every
Breeze, wind, bluster, gale and storm
Notates its own chimes.

                                    Sometimes they echo
                            Faintly, like church bells calling
                                        From a drowned village.

Occasionally
A tintinnabulation
Cascades from the branch.

In knotted silence
After a storm they plead for
Tuneful untangling.

The recurrent note
That plays even in silence
Is my gratitude.

I'll send a goldfinch
To hear them, knowing they do
Not now toll for me.

Soon now their chiming
Will charm the bud from the branch
The leaf from the bud.

Meditation Bowl

From a tourist shop,
Yes, but strike the bowl, gently,
And it still rings true.

> Strike the bowl, gently,
> To release Himalayan
> Reverberations.

Strike the bowl, gently.
The echoes will gleam for now
And ever after.

> Strike the bowl, gently,
> To understand that what goes
> Around comes around.

Dream yourself into
The music of the spheres, then
Strike the bowl, gently.

> Strike the bowl, gently,
> To feel the air ripple towards
> Concelebration.

If you would believe
What is far beyond belief
Strike the bowl, gently.

www.ingramcontent.com/pod-product-compliance
Lightning Source LLC
Chambersburg PA
CBHW030500100426
42813CB00002B/295